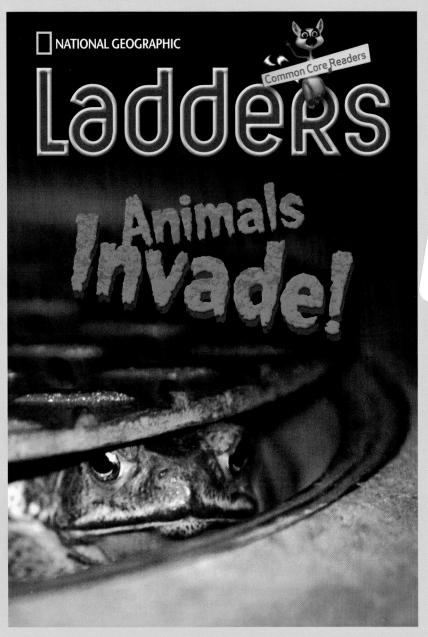

NATIONAL GEOGRAPHIC

Ladders

Common Core Readers

Animals Invade!

Invasive Species EVERYWHERE!

by Barbara Wood
illustrated by Clare Nichols

The world was perfect long ago.
Each species had its place.
The **predators** and preyed upon
Lived in a balanced space.

Till someone picked the whole world up
And shook it all around,
Then stopped—and all the animals
Came tumbling to the ground.

Some landed here, some landed there,
In corners of the earth
Where they had never been before,
And then some pairs gave birth.

The babies grew and had some more,
Soon there were quite a lot.
Competing, eating all the food
The **native** species sought.

Invasive species everywhere,
And **habitats** askew!*
So learn a lesson from the act
That we have come to rue.*

Before you give the world a shake,
Consider what you do.
Each action has a **consequence**
And **chaos** may ensue.*

*askew   twisted the wrong way
*rue   regret
*ensue   happen as a result

Check In What lesson does this poem teach?

3

Toad-al!

Millions of giant, warty toads are invading neighborhoods, destroying homes, stealing food, and harming those who try to stop them. It might sound like a scary movie, but for many animals in Australia, it's a fact of life. Cane toads are harming **native** animals by invading their **habitats,** eating their food, and even killing some animals.

The cane toad is an **invasive species.** An invasive species is a living being that does not belong in a place and can harm the environment. Many invasive species arrive in a new habitat by accident. Others, however, are brought to a new habitat on purpose.

Cane toad

Takeover

by Susan Halko

New Toad = New Trouble

Cane toads are native to Central and South America, but were brought to Australia to solve a problem. In 1935, about 100 toads were shipped to Australia to eat beetles that were destroying sugarcane crops. That's how the cane toad got its name. An entomologist, a scientist who studies insects, had warned against introducing the cane toad. The entomologist's name was W.W. Froggatt, and he was right. Instead of getting rid of the pests, the toads themselves became pests. They ate everything except cane beetles. Today, there are hundreds of millions of cane toads eating their way across Australia.

Cane beetle
on sugarcane

One Tough Toad

As far as toads go, cane toads are giant-sized. In fact, they are the largest toads in the world. They can be up to 24 centimeters (9 inches) long and weigh up to 2 kilograms (4.4 pounds). You'd need both hands to hold a big cane toad.

Poison Gland
A gland above each shoulder produces white poison. This close-up is magnified.

Bony Ridge
Cane toads have bony ridges on their face.

Feet
The front feet have separate toes. Cane toads can use the feet for digging.

Cane toads also have a secret weapon to help in their invasion—poison **glands.** If an animal, such as a lizard, a snake, or even a crocodile, tries to eat a cane toad, a poisonous spray oozes from the glands. The cane toad's poison is so strong that it can kill an animal in minutes. If a person triggers a cane toad's poison glands, he or she might experience intense pain or a short period of blindness. Even the eggs of the cane toad are poisonous and if eaten, can cause death.

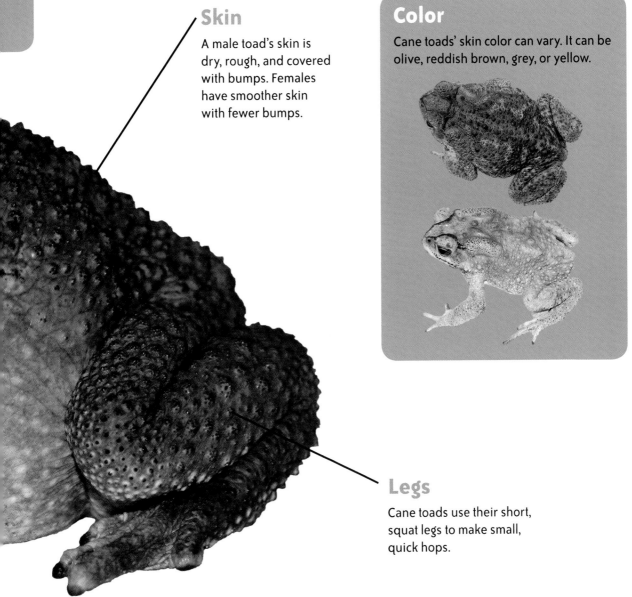

Skin

A male toad's skin is dry, rough, and covered with bumps. Females have smoother skin with fewer bumps.

Color

Cane toads' skin color can vary. It can be olive, reddish brown, grey, or yellow.

Legs

Cane toads use their short, squat legs to make small, quick hops.

Land of Opportunity

Another reason the cane toad population has taken over its new habitat is that cane toads have few **predators** in Australia. In Central and South America, animals eat cane toads. Parasites and diseases there also control the cane toad population. But in Australia, parasites and diseases have little impact on cane toads. The road is wide open for the spread of the cane toad population.

Cane toads need a lot of food to survive. They have
learned different ways to find food in their new
habitat. At night, cane toads gather in large, open areas.
There, they are able to see mice, small lizards, and
other moving targets. They gather under streetlights
to wait for insects that are attracted to the light. They
hide under porches, in cans, or under rocks and then
ambush their prey. They have even been known to
steal dog food that has been left outside.

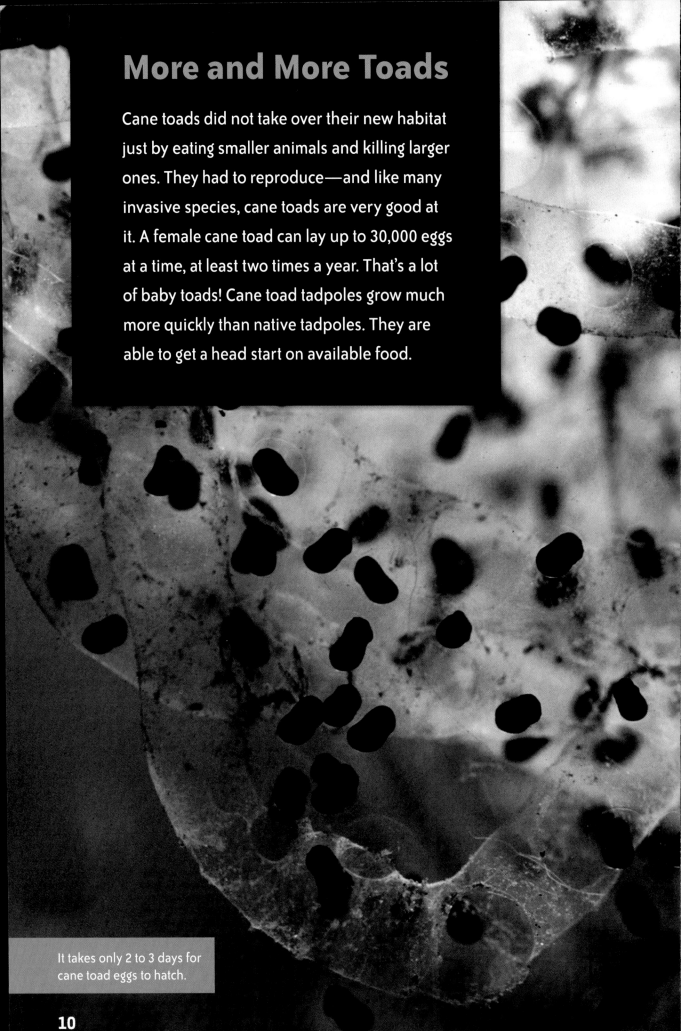

More and More Toads

Cane toads did not take over their new habitat just by eating smaller animals and killing larger ones. They had to reproduce—and like many invasive species, cane toads are very good at it. A female cane toad can lay up to 30,000 eggs at a time, at least two times a year. That's a lot of baby toads! Cane toad tadpoles grow much more quickly than native tadpoles. They are able to get a head start on available food.

It takes only 2 to 3 days for cane toad eggs to hatch.

Super Adapter

Cane toads have also **adapted** to their new habitat. Although they thrive in wet, tropical environments, they can store water to survive on dry land. And although they prefer warmer temperatures, they can survive in temperatures as low as 5°C (41°F). This climate is different than that of their native habitat.

Scientists have even found that today's cane toads have legs that are about 10 percent longer than earlier generations of cane toads. This adaptation has helped the toads spread into new areas more quickly.

A Growing Threat

Shortly after their invasion of Australia began, the cane toad population spread at a rate of about 10 kilometers (6 miles) a year. Now, their population is spreading at a rate of about 50 kilometers (30 miles) a year, and the land they inhabit is about the size of Texas, Oklahoma, and Louisiana combined!

Scientists think that some native animals may be developing ways to survive alongside the toad. Red-bellied snakes may now have smaller heads and jaws than in the past. This adaptation prevents the snakes from eating the poisonous toads. Some birds have learned to turn the toads over before eating them to avoid the poison glands.

With their huge appetite, poison, lack of predators, and ability to adapt and reproduce, cane toads seem unstoppable. Researchers are working to find a parasite that can kill cane toads without harming native animals. Volunteers collect eggs and toads, and set traps. Still, the cane toad invasion continues.

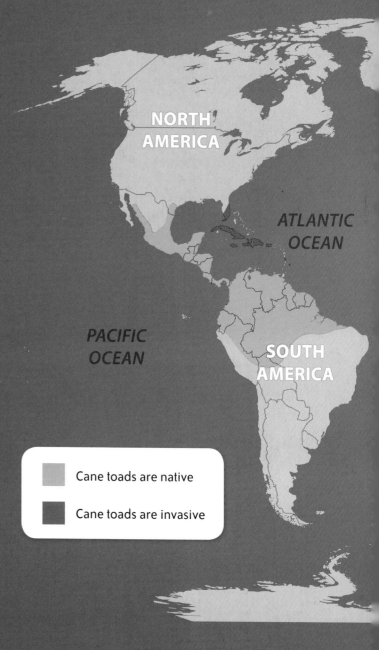

Cane Toad Range

NORTH AMERICA

ATLANTIC OCEAN

PACIFIC OCEAN

SOUTH AMERICA

Cane toads are native

Cane toads are invasive

The red-bellied black snake may be adapting to live with the toad.

This bird is called a whistling kite. It can eat cane toads and survive.

ARCTIC OCEAN

EUROPE

ASIA

PACIFIC OCEAN

AFRICA

INDIAN OCEAN

OCEANIA

AUSTRALIA

ANTARCTICA

Check In What are some reasons the cane toad continues to thrive in nonnative habitats?

Lila's Smile

by Hilary Wagner | Illustrated by Will Terry

If ever there was a time in a young cane toad's life when a decision needed to be made, this was that time. Lila gazed at the boat swaying gently in the water. It was a red and white vessel with a high bow and sturdy sides that seemed confident and ready to tackle the waves in the open sea beyond the dock. Lila couldn't help but stare at a thick rope that hung over the bow and at the two life preservers above it. It looked as though the boat were smiling at her.

The boat belonged to a man with rich caramel-colored skin, dressed in fine clothes. He and his crew spoke in a language Lila had never heard before, with words that seemed to roll off their tongues like music. The man and his crew had gone to speak with the local farmers, returning with brown burlap sacks filled with grain or maybe seeds, and then going back for more. The man had an agreeable smile and a spindly mustache and spoke softly to his crew. Lila liked that.

Lila hopped over to an older
toad who was sitting in the brush
watching the boat. A crew member
saw her, but continued going about his
business. "Where do you think the boat is
from?" Lila asked the old toad.

"Well," replied the toad, "it most certainly is
not from here. If any human from this land had
seen you, he'd have been after you in a second."
Then he smiled and stared off past the shoreline. "I wonder . . ."

"What do you wonder?" asked Lila, her eyes widening
with curiosity.

"I wonder if that boat is from South America," replied the
toad. "It's a lovely place, far away from here, where cane toads
are welcome . . . our homeland."

Lila had heard of that place before . . . *South America*.
Her grandfather had spoken of it once, he too with a
smile on his face. "Have you ever been there?"

"Why, yes," replied the old toad. "We were taken from South America and brought here."

"My grandfather came from there, too," said Lila, "long before I was born."

The old toad leaned in, inspecting Lila's face, squinting at her. "Ah, yes," he said. "I'm afraid my eyesight is waning in my old age. In my younger days I would have noticed that dappled green pattern right away. Your grandfather was Santos, wasn't he?" Lila nodded. "Santos and I, and many others, were brought here from South America, forced to leave our homeland." The toad motioned to the men walking on and off the boat. "Those men, they remind me very much of South America. We seldom saw humans there, but when we did, they spoke like that. And they didn't despise us or hunt us."

"Why did the humans bring us here?" asked Lila.

"To eat the beetles that destroy their precious sugarcane crops. The humans didn't bother to ask us first, or to find out whether we eat those beetles," answered the old toad. "We don't! It's easy to find other things to eat here, though, so in many ways we are thriving. But it's clear we're not welcome here. I dearly wish we could return to our **native** land."

"Well then, why don't we do that?" asked Lila. That seemed to be a logical solution to the dilemma.

With a heavy sigh, the old toad gazed at Lila with compassionate eyes. "And how might we do that, young lass? We are mere toads after all." He set a gentle webbed hand on Lila's shoulder. "Do yourself a favor, my dear, and give up silly dreams." Slowly, the old toad hopped away into in the brush.

Lila thought of what the old toad had told her, how in South America cane toads were welcome, not thought of as an **invasive species** as they were here. Here they were known only as pests, a term Lila did not care for. Never having asked to come here, she didn't like being thought of as a pest or invasive.

Lila knew that cane toads were venomous creatures, and when they grew afraid or landed into trouble, a deadly poison oozed from their skin. The thought of hurting another living being of any kind saddened Lila. She didn't want to hurt anyone. None of the cane toads did.

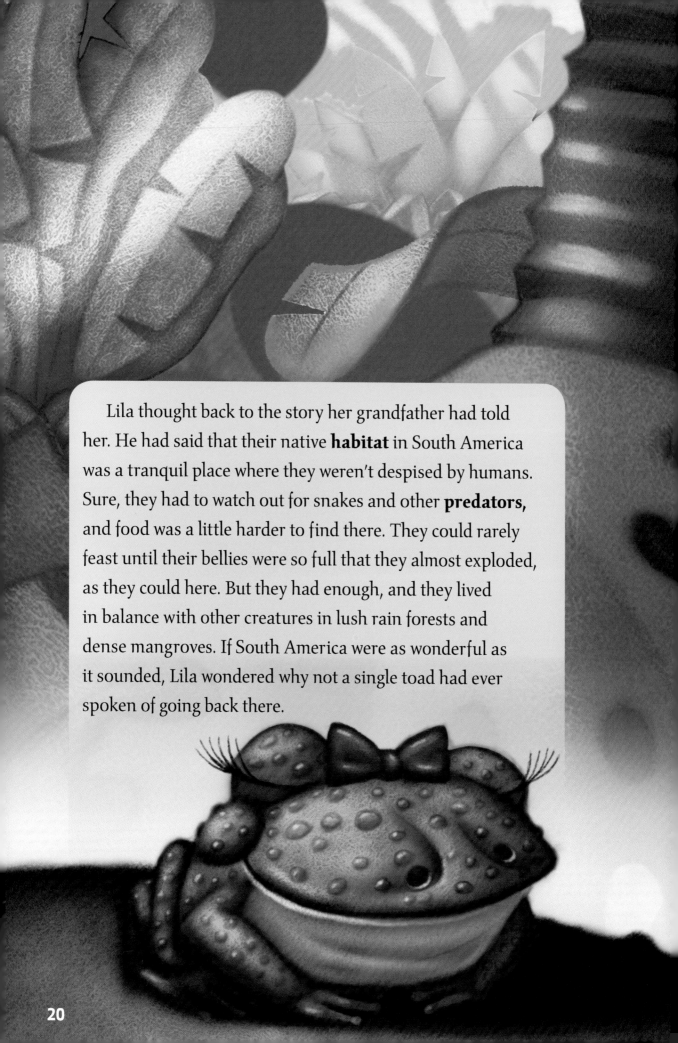

Lila thought back to the story her grandfather had told her. He had said that their native **habitat** in South America was a tranquil place where they weren't despised by humans. Sure, they had to watch out for snakes and other **predators,** and food was a little harder to find there. They could rarely feast until their bellies were so full that they almost exploded, as they could here. But they had enough, and they lived in balance with other creatures in lush rain forests and dense mangroves. If South America were as wonderful as it sounded, Lila wondered why not a single toad had ever spoken of going back there.

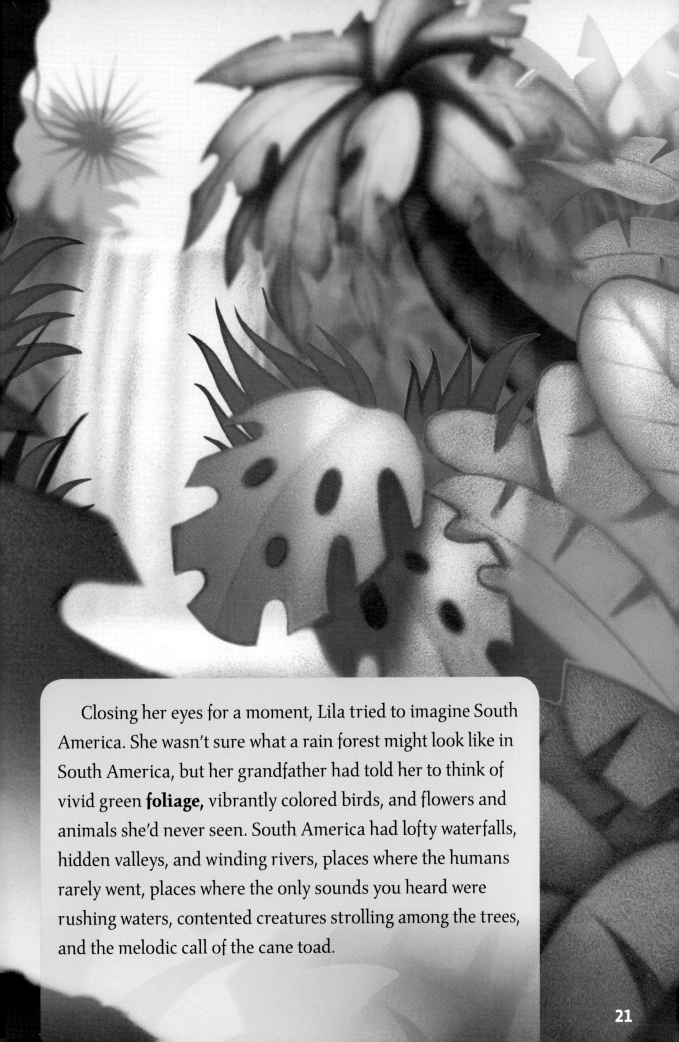

Closing her eyes for a moment, Lila tried to imagine South America. She wasn't sure what a rain forest might look like in South America, but her grandfather had told her to think of vivid green **foliage,** vibrantly colored birds, and flowers and animals she'd never seen. South America had lofty waterfalls, hidden valleys, and winding rivers, places where the humans rarely went, places where the only sounds you heard were rushing waters, contented creatures strolling among the trees, and the melodic call of the cane toad.

Lila wondered if the cane toads' call was as lovely as her grandfather had claimed it to be. She'd never heard it in the woods, at least not in the way her grandfather had described it. Since they'd arrived here, the cane toads agreed to stay quiet. If humans could not hear them, they were far more likely to survive. Her grandfather described the cane toad call as a rhythmic sequence of throaty clicks that carried through the trees like a musical sort of wind. Once one toad began the call, the others joined in, creating a stunning symphony of harmonious clicks and clacks, a masterpiece of sound.

Sighing miserably, Lila opened her eyes, watching as the crew continued to load the boat. She wondered where the boat might be going. She would like to go away, to slip aboard that boat and go to her homeland. Perhaps in her real habitat, she would hear the mysterious call of the cane toad. The old toad said the humans from the boat sounded just like the humans from South America. What if they were from South America? What if that boat would soon be setting sail for the emerald rain forests and rushing waterfalls? Lila marveled at the thought.

Lila's father was her only real family left, and he had recently taken to the deep woodlands to hide, due to rumors that humans were planning another massive cane toad **cull.** He suggested that Lila do the same. Lila wanted to find her father and ask him some questions. After watching the boat and speaking to the old toad, there was an important decision to be made, and she needed her father's advice.

Lila's father, Angus, was by and large a sensible toad. Lila knew this well. After all, her father was still alive, having survived the cull that claimed Lila's mother's life when Lila was just a tadpole. It took a lot to survive in a land where no one seemed to want you.

Lila spotted Angus sitting in the hollow of his favorite tree. "Father," croaked Lila, "I need to speak with you."

"Not so loud," whispered her father anxiously. "What if an enemy is close at hand?"

"Sorry," replied Lila. "I only wanted to see you."

"It's all right," said her father, patting Lila's small head, "but you need to stop taking so many chances. A toad only gets one life, you know."

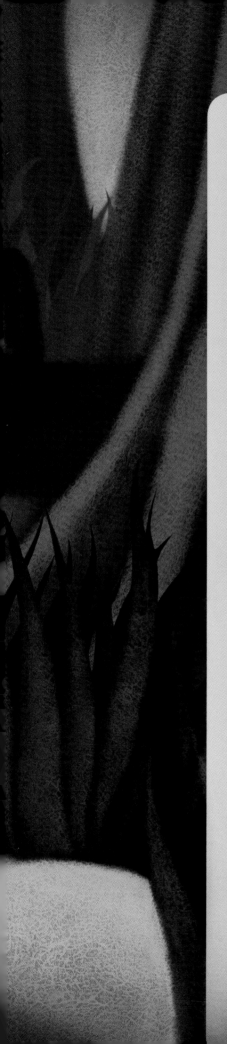

"I know, Father," said Lila. "That's why I've come to find you. I need to ask you about something that's been weighing on my mind."

"Oh," said her father in an inquisitive tone. "What do you want to know about, Lila— maneuvers to help you wriggle from the grip of a human hand?"

"No," replied Lila, shaking her head, "nothing like that." She crinkled up her face, thinking how to suitably word her question. "Actually, I wanted to ask you about the many boats that come to shore. Why haven't you, or any other cane toads for that matter, ever slipped aboard one? Perhaps we could find our way back home . . . to South America."

Cocking his head in a probing manner, Angus spoke to his daughter in a grave tone. "Why, that is simply not a sensible plan, Lila, taking such chances. What if that boat took us somewhere cold and snowy, or to a place with predators that aren't harmed by the poison that protects us? Here, we have few predators and we find plenty to eat. We've gotten used to the easy life. You could say we're thriving—as long as humans aren't afoot."

Lila considered her father's answer, which made good sense. Still, humans were determined to eradicate them, and living in fear of the next cull didn't seem like much of a life.

Lila looked down glumly, staring at the wet grass beneath her feet. She remembered the smile on the old toad's face when he spoke of their homeland. Her grandfather wore that same smile when he spoke of South America. Thinking on it, Lila couldn't remember seeing smiles like that very often in this place. In fact she'd never seen her father smile like that, not ever. "Sensible or not, I'm willing to take that chance," she said resolutely.

"My child," said Lila's father firmly, "you need to stay deep in the woodlands with me and hide. That way you'll always be sure to survive."

Lila thought of the smiling man and his spindly mustache. He'd soon be leaving on his boat, sailing back to whatever distant land he came from. She thought about surviving, as her father had put it, and what that word meant. "Father, I don't want to merely survive. Hiding in the woodlands for the rest of my life may allow me to survive, but I want more. I want to live." She thought of the rain forest and the cane toads' call. "I want to find my smile. I think you want to find yours, too, and neither of us will find our smiles hiding in the woodlands." Saying nothing in response, Angus stared at his daughter in utter astonishment.

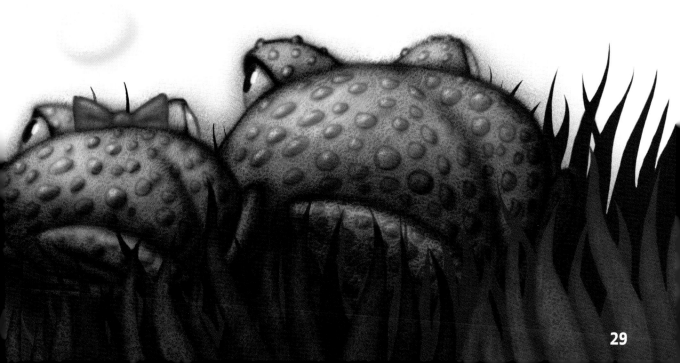

After the sun had set and the moon had risen, Lila and her father sat on the shore and watched as the last of the crew went aboard the boat, guided by lanterns.

"Are you ready?" asked Angus. "Once we hop onto that boat, there will be no turning back—ever."

Lila peered over her shoulder, inspecting the darkening brush. She listened for the melodic calls of her fellow cane toads, but she did not hear them.

"Yes, Father, I'm ready," replied Lila.

Lila and her father hopped silently aboard the boat. Despite their caution, a crew member saw the toads, but seemed unconcerned and went about his business.

After endless days at sea, they finally arrived on a sandy shore. It was lined with towering palm trees and abundant, colorful foliage. Oddly colored fruits grew from the trees and bushes, and the mangroves were fuller and greener than any mangrove Lila had ever seen.

Lila's ears perked. "Do you hear that?"

"Yes," Angus replied, his eyes widening.

Lila gasped. "I never thought I'd hear it—the call of the cane toad!"

Without a sound, the toads hopped off the boat, both of them smiling. Lila turned back for a moment and gazed at the boat. It seemed to be smiling, too.

Check In Why is it important for Lila to find her smile?

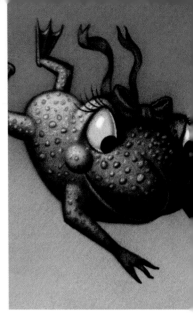

Discuss | Compare Text Structure

1. Explain the differences between a poem, such as "Invasive Species Everywhere," and a story. What elements does a poem have that a story does not have?

2. What was the cause of the cane toad problem in Australia?

3. What was the effect of bringing cane toads to Australia?

4. Imagine writing a fiction story about cane toads. Would the cane toads in your story be likable, like Lila, or not? Explain why.

5. What do you still wonder about invasive species? What else would you like to know?